G000153713

ONE RING ZERO

AS SMART AS WE ARE

PUBLISHED BY
SOFT SKULL PRESS
71 BOND STREET
BROOKLYN, NY 11217
WWW.SOFTSKULL.COM

DISTRIBUTED TO THE BOOK TRADE BY PGW

PACKAGED BY sockit projects

DESIGNED BY HONEST

LIBRARY OF CONGRESS CATALOGING-IN-PUBLICATION DATA AVAILABLE.

ISBN 1-932360-42-5
PRINTED IN CHINA

10 9 8 7 6 5 4 3 2 1

TABLE OF CONTENTS

A BRIEF HISTORY OF ONE RING ZERO BY DIMITRI EHRLICH

Michael Hearst and Joshua Camp met in 1995, while working at the Hohner musical instrument warehouse and repair center in Richmond, Virginia. There, as Hearst tuned harmonicas eight hours a day while Camp worked as an accordion technician, the two developed a friendship based on a shared interest in oddball instruments. The Hohner factory in Germany would occasionally send over prototypes of strange musical instruments that never caught on—such as the claviola, a modified accordion that you blow into to produce sound—and Hearst and Camp soon came up with the idea of forming a band based on one-of-a-kind instruments that few other musicians had ever heard of, much less learned to play. Thus was born One Ring Zero, a duo that occasionally swells to a sextet and specializes in the sort of 19th-century, gypsy-klezmer, circus-flea-cartoon music you mainly hear in your dreams.

Two years ago, after receiving the sort of micro-acclaim sometimes accorded to artists whose chosen genres doom them to a fetishist's obscurity, One Ring Zero decided they'd gotten as big as instrumental avant-klezmatics could in Richmond, Virginia, and headed north to New York. Walking down the street in Brooklyn one day, Hearst dropped into a bookstore (called simply, Store), which Dave Eggers had created as an outlet for his publishing company, McSweeney's. Hearst offered the store manager a copy of his band's CD. Within a month, One Ring Zero was McSweeney's house band, accompanying New York's literary stars during weekly readings.

It was at Store that One Ring Zero met author Rick Moody, who, after hearing them play, asked them to perform with him during readings. "We felt it was only fair to turn the tables," Hearst said, "and ask Rick to write lyrics for us." Unwittingly, One Ring Zero had stumbled on an entirely new direction: an album of songs with lyrics specifically written for them by their favorite authors. Here, a conversation with Hearst and Camp about how *As Smart As We Are*—their fifth album so far—has taken them to the farthest frontiers of Lit Rock wilderness, and what the weather's like there.

Dimitri Ehrlich: What does a claviola look like?

Michael Hearst: Kind of looks like a swan that's been run over by a car. It's got one wing that sticks out and it's got this curved neck that you blow into. You wear it like an accordion, but you only have the right-hand keys.

DE: You guys love to use odd instruments. What are your favorites?

MH: Our studio is just littered with random toys. We have all the standard stuff—drums, bass, and guitars, but we also tend to use anything in the room, whether it's the water pipes or a power drill, a theremin, claviola, slide whistle, Mega-Mouth—things like that.

DE: What's a Mega-Mouth?

MH: Mega-Mouth is this little toy that Joshua found at a closeout at Kaybee Toys. It's like a small vocoder, but there were like five different versions and they were being sold for a dollar a piece. They have this really horrible sound quality that we love to use. We've also done stuff like put a microphone up to the electric meter in the basement and use that as a drone behind a song. Then there's the bread machine. Once, we let it run on its cycle and used that as the rhythm track.

Joshua Camp: And we like to run everything through inexpensive pedals. Not good ones. Like the Ibanez chorus pedal from 1984.

MH: We'll take the theremin and run it through a vibrato, a reverb, and an old analog delay unit and get some ridiculous sounds. The backing tracks in Daniel Handler's song went through every pedal we own.

JC: For this project we used our entire bag of tricks.

DE: How does it impact a band to get your big break playing at a literary event?

MH: When we got to the McSweeney's store it was when their reading series was just beginning, and their store was about eight feet wide by sixteen feet long. They'd get these amazing people like Viggo Mortensen and A.M. Homes to read in the store and would fit all of fifteen people in there sweating, crammed together. It was kind of like the 40 Watt Club in Athens, the original one with one light bulb. That was the beginning of the series. It eventually moved on to Galapagos where we had an audience of two hundred people practically every time. But this was the real beginning of that whole thing and where we got to know a lot of the authors.

DE: Did you play while they were reading, or in between?

MH: It was just us, essentially playing in between readings or even opening the set up with a few songs. We'd play a couple One Ring Zero songs and then the readings would begin. Then it was Rick Moody who first asked us if we wanted to play behind him and improvise while he read. It worked out so well that Rick asked if we would record some of the music. We did the opening chapter to **Purple America**.

DE: What is it like to take the words of a renowned writer and set them to music? What are some of the challenges?

JC: I think the challenge of making songs out of words that aren't necessarily straightforward lyrics is how to make them musical. This whole process leads you into unconventional song forms, which I like a lot. You end up writing a song in a form that you'd never think of on your own, because normally you tend to go back to the basic sort of verse-chorus-bridge structures that you know work. Some of these songs are quite obviously not in that structure and I think in the end the songs are more interesting because of it.

DE: One Ring Zero has been described in the press as "Lit Rock." Is that a legit musical genre?

MH: What the hell is Lit Rock?

JC: What makes it Lit Rock is that people recognize the names of the people who wrote the lyrics. Otherwise this record is a pop record. It may be a little quirkier than Britney Spears, but it's still a pop record.

DE: Do you have any good backstage stories?

MH: I don't think we've ever played a place that had a backstage.

JC: When we play a place that has a backstage we'll let you know.

FIONA MAAZEL
HEAD NOTES

The title *As Smart as We Are* beat out several contenders, among them Chapter 11, Books Are Boring, and, my favorite, Some of Our Friends Are Famous. I can just imagine the guys who make it happen—Michael Hearst and Joshua Camp—molting in the basement gulag where they record, tossing out names with increased urgency. Titles are a tricky business. Jonathan Lethem once said in a *Paris Review* interview that a good title has to satisfy three criteria: eye feel, mouth feel, and the before and after effect, meaning that the title has to make sense on its own, and also deepen or complicate the novel after you've read it. *As Smart as We Are* is sort of hilarious on this last count, given the roster of talent One Ring Zero has managed to put together for the project. As smart as we are, we're still writing lyrics. But also, as smart as we are, we're attempting to write lyrics, which is actually not an easy proposition. And lastly, from ORZ's vantage, as smart as we are, it's still pretty ballsy to score seventeen songs for seventeen writers who might never have heard of you and who, in all likelihood, have not written lyrics before, but who sure as hell do now. And without hesitation. Ask a writer to immortalize himself in song and it's a done deal. As the truism goes: Every writer wants to be a rock star. Could be because a lot of us are captive to solitude, shy and undersexed, and self-hating to a degree that wants to be paraded on stage, but can't. Or maybe it's just that the writer-rocker combination is hot. At the very least, lyricizing gives an author the chance to vent gimmick, rhyme, alliteration, froth—in short, the very things that can compromise a good piece of fiction. Most every writer I know has destructive impulses toward excess, be it heart, humor, sincerity, dialogue. The writer Ken Kalfus frequently refers to his first round on a story as the vomit draft. Hemingway once said that the sentences you love best are typically the ones that need to get axed.

INTRODUCTION

PAUL AUSTER
NATTY MAN BLUES

2

THERE AIN'T NO SIN IN CINCINNATI

SINCE I BEEN IN CINCINNATI
I GOTTA GET OUT OF CINCINNATI

OR ELSE I'LL GO PLUMB DUMB AND BATTY

SINCE I MEAN TO SIN WHEREVER I AM
SINCE I MEAN TO SIN WHENEVER I CAN

I'LL CROSS THE RIVER INTO OLD KENTUCK
FIND ME SOME SKIRT AND A CHANGE OF LUCK

DRINK SOME SHOTS AND ROLL IN THE MUCK
RAISE SOME HELL AND REMEMBER TO DUCK

SINCE I MEAN TO SIN WHEREVER I AM
SINCE I MEAN TO SIN WHENEVER I CAN

THERE AIN'T NO SIN IN CINCINNATI
SINCE I BEEN IN CINCINNATI

ITS FACE AIN'T NATTY AND ITS HEART IS RATT

SO I GOTTA GET OUT OF CINCINNATI

SINCE I MEAN TO SIN WHEREVER I A

SINCE I MEAN TO SIN WHENEVER I CA

I would not be surprised if one of those lines were "There ain't no sin in Cincinnati." There's a name for that sort of thing besides **irony**, some underused Latinate term, not **homophone**, but maybe **aphesis**, though that suggests **sin** actually derives from **Cincinnati**, which is just wrong, if amusing. Well, who cares. Point is, it sounds good–that internal echo–and is fun in a way that perhaps Auster's **The Invention of Solitude** would not tolerate. Likewise with "plumb dumb and batty," though who doesn't want to say that on a regular basis? It's got mouth feel all right. Plumb dumb, plumb dumb, plumb dumb.

3 DANIEL HANDLER
RADIO

IF I HAD A RADIO FOR EVERY TIME YOU LOVED ME SO,
I WOULDN'T HAVE A RADIO AT ALL.
NOW I SIT AND WASTE MY TIME, MY ROOM AS QUIET AS A MIME,
AND WAIT FOR SOMEONE GLAMOROUS TO CALL.

RADIO, RADIO, RADIO, RADIO, RADIO.

IF I HAD A CEILING FAN FOR EVERY TIME YOU MADE A PLAN,
THEN TOLD ME YOU HAD PLANS AND COULDN'T GO,
THE HURRICANE WOULD WRECK MY BED AND LEAVE MY SHINGLED ROOF FOR DEAD,
AND MY BROKEN HEART WOULD SCATTER TO AND FRO.

HURRICANE, HURRICANE, HURRICANE, HURRICANE, HURRICANE.

IF I HAD A LEISURE SUIT ONE TENTH OF ONE PERCENT AS CUTE
AS CERTAIN PARTS OF ASPECTS OF YOUR FACE,
EVERY SINGLE SUMMER DAY I'D LOOK SO FUCKING GOOD YOU'D SAY,
"THE WAY I TREATED YOU WAS A DISGRACE.

FUCKING GOOD, FUCKING GOOD, FUCKING GOOD, FUCKING GOOD,
I WISH I HAD A RADIO WITH SONGS ABOUT YOU.

Fucking good. As a refrain, it's not nearly as aural as plumb dumb—less fragile,
easier on the lips—but it's still the thing we'd rather say. Over and over. Especially
given the loopy claviola line that precedes it. But that's Daniel Handler's thing: grit
and cheek. As the rumor goes, he's responsible for the grimmest children's books ever.

I'M LEAVING YOU TODAY
WHAT'S THAT YOU SAY?
OKAY?
I'M SERIOUS THIS TIME
UNLESS YOU MIND

D'YOU MIND? D'YOU MIND? D'YOU MIND?
PLEASE MIND

I'M SURE YOU NEED ME NOW MAKE THINGS EASY
COULDN'T YOU SAY IT TO PLEASE ME, JUST THIS TIME?
I'M HALFWAY DOWN THE STREET
GUESS THIS IS IT.
IS IT?
I'D STILL BE YOUR MAN: THINK I CAN.

DON'T LAUGH. DON'T LAUGH. DON'T LAUGH.
WHY'D YOU LAUGH?

I'M SURE YOU, IN FACT, LOVE ME
I TRUST YOU, IN FACT, CARE
I KNOW THAT YOU COULD LOVE ME, IF YOU DARE

Point being: No one can escape his predilections. Witness Darin Strauss, author of **Chang and Eng,** who's obviously got a penchant for doubles, doppelgangers, and, in this case, the double that is not: I love you! You love me! Oh, hopeless. Then again, the music smokes out the comedy of need—the tremolo laid down over the chorus, the puppet theater of the last stanza, the theremin wiggle at the end. Ha, ha, you're lonely, let's make a ditty.

5

RICK MOODY
KISS ME, YOU BRAT

KISS ME, YOU BRAT

DON'T MAKE ME ASK
STARS IN THE NIGHT
SKY

DON'T ASK TO SHINE
DO THEY?

KISS ME, YOU FOOL
DON'T MAKE ME KNEEL
BLOOMS ON THE ROSEBUSH
DON'T STOOP TO KNEEL
WHEN IT'S SPRING

"Kiss Me, You Brat" is the only song on the album whose lyrics were written after the music, which argues for the way word and sound can galvanize each other. I'm thinking of writers who often have the cadence of a sentence in mind before the words, and whose prose, as a result, is lucid and melodious. There's a reason most writers are asked what they listen to. It's like asking Michael Jordan what he eats for breakfast. Leonard Bernstein makes an interesting case for this in his Norton Lectures, by way of twinning linguistic theory with music theory, e.g., plumb dumb vis-à-vis the dum dum dah dum of Beethoven's Ninth.

LAWRENCE KRAUSER
DEPOSTION DISPOSITION

SALLY DIDN'T DO IT
SHE SWEARS SHE DIDN'T DO IT
SHE DOESN'T EVEN HAVE TO
THE TRUTH WILL DO THE TALKING

NEIGHBORS THOUGHT SHE DID IT
LEAST SHE THOUGHT THEY THOUGHT SO
NOT THAT THEY PROFILED
BUT SHE
WOULD FIT EXACTLY

THE DAY SHE MOVED TO TOWN
THAT NIGHT WAS WHEN IT HAPPENED
THE HANDPRINT ON THE WINDOW
WILL CLEAR ME

AND SHE NEVER THOUGHT SHE DID IT
NOT EVEN FOR ONE SECOND
FOR INDEED SHE HADN'T DONE IT
BUT SHE FELT LIKE SHE HAD DONE IT

SHE WAS SURE THAT HOW SHE FELT
WAS EXACTLY HOW SHE'D FEEL
WHICH SHE HADN'T
THAT THESE FEELINGS WERE THOSE FEELINGS
THE OFFICERS WERE FRIENDLY
NOT ONE FINGER POINTED
WHY ON EARTH WOULD EVER SHE
PERP HAND THRUST THROUGH OPEN WINDOW

NO ONE EVEN EVER ENTERED
I'M A PILLAR OF SOCIETY
ALBEIT PLANTED YESTERDAY

PEDAL PRINTS THROUGH BACKYARD MUD
THOSE ARE NOT MY FOOTPRINTS
INNOCENCE IS THE BEST DEFENSE
REALTOR CALLED TO FOLLOW UP
FRESH PIE AT THE DOOR

SALLY VERY SORRY
NEVER MEANT NO HARM
AND NEVER DONE A THING

TO MAKE NONE

Which accounts, loosely, for the call and response of Lawrence Krauser's song. Ping-pong, depose, dispose, they are kind of the same thing. Deposition, disposition are too, which is why the call-response on this tune is so apt. And funny. Funny in the way language always returns to its music, which starts when we're children gagging on a hunk of tuna.

7

CLAY MCLEOD CHAPMAN
HALF AND HALF

EVER SINCE THE DAY I WAS BORN-
SOMETHING SET ME APART.

MY MOTHER TOOK ONE LOOK AT ME
AND I NEARLY BROKE HER HEART.

HALF AND HALF.
GO AHEAD AND JUST DO THE MATH.
I WAS BORN UNDER GOD'S OWN WRATH. I WAS BORN HALF AND HALF.

HALF AND HALF.
ALL THE MEN - THEY'RE GOING DAFT.
THEY CAN'T COMPETE WITH MY OWN STAFF.
I WAS BORN HALF AND HALF.

MY FATHER WOULDN'T LOOK AT ME,
TREATING ME LIKE A CHURL .
HE ALWAYS WONDERED IF I WAS HIS SON
OR DADDY'S LITTLE GIRL.

HALF AND HALF.
GO AHEAD AND JUST GIVE A LAUGH.
THE GIRLS ALL SWOON WHEN I CROSS THEIR PATH.
I WAS BORN HALF AND HALF

It's the human scale. And on it, towards the middle, is number six of one, half a dozen of the other, a song in equal parts, tits and bits. Incidentally, the name *Hermaphroditus* was given the son of Hermes and Aphrodite *before* he became both man and woman. As if the conflation, that trick of language, determined his outcome. It's a chicken-egg moment: words, music.

DAVE EGGERS
THE GHOST OF RITA GONZALO

IF I WERE A VOLCANO, I WOULD WANT YOU TO JUMP.
JUMP INTO MY YELLOW.
JUMP INTO MY HOT YELLOW.
YOU PERSON MADE OF BONES.

IF I WERE A WELL I WOULD WANT YOU TO YELL DOWN MY DEPTHS
YOUR VOICE BOOMING,
ECHOING
MY WELL IS DEEP AND BLACK

PEOPLE DRIVE CARS ALONE
MOST PEOPLE ARE ALONE WHEN THEY DRIVE
THEY SING WHEN THEY DRIVE
BECAUSE THEY'RE ALONE WITH THEIR HANDS

WHEN PEOPLE SING WHEN ALONE
PEOPLE FIND THEM WRETCHED
PEOPLE FIND THEM DISGUSTING
THIS HAPPENS IN EVERY PART OF THE WORLD

"When people sing when alone, people find them wretched," reminds me of a favorite line from Donald Antrim's *The Verificationist*: "Have you ever noticed?—people, no matter how beautiful or desirable, invariably will, if observed closely while going about their daily business of keeping alive, begin to seem like monsters." Never mind that the hero of this song actually wants something called a "hot yellow," which, even in volcano terms, is rather lewd.

MARGARET ATWOOD
FRANKENSTEIN MONSTER SONG

I'M NINE FEET TALL AND MY SKIN IS GREY,
ALL THE GIRLS SCREAM WHEN I COME OUT TO PLAY -
THEY SCREAM AND THEY SCREAM AND THEY RUN AWAY-

I'M ONE OF A KIND.

DOCTOR, DOCTOR, YOU'RE THE ONE TO BLAME,
YOU PUT ME TOGETHER, YOU FORGOT THE NAME.
SEW ME A LADY.
SEW ME A LADY.
SEW ME A MONSTER LADY JUST LIKE ME.

I'VE GOT A DEAD MAN'S HEART AND A DEAD MAN'S BRAIN.
I LOOK IN THE MIRROR AND IT'S PURE PAIN.
I'M SO UGLY AND SO LONELY THAT I'M GOING INSANE,
OUT OF MY MIND.

DOCTOR, DOCTOR, PLEASE, USE ALL YOUR ART
MAKE ME A GIRL WITH A DEAD GIRL'S HEART -
SEW ME A LADY.
SEW ME A LADY -
SEW ME A MONSTER LADY JUST LIKE ME.

Which brings us to the lonely monster, Mary Shelley's prototype long since domesticated by the aesthetics of charity—the ugly duckling, the death-row guy, Beauty and the Beast, the Elephant Man. Atwood's monster is no different. He needs a good lay and some coco-butter emollient. As for Atwood, it makes sense that she'd assimilate the freak for ORZ lyrics. After all, people have assimilated her work left and right. Remember how *the* line from *The Handmaid's Tale* ("don't let the bastards get you down") makes a modified cameo in that U2 song, "Acrobat"? Or how a lot of singers, especially Bono, lift phrases from stuff they've read, e.g., "In dreams begin responsibilities" (also in "Acrobat") from Delmore Schwartz's short story of that title, though maybe he got it from Yeats.

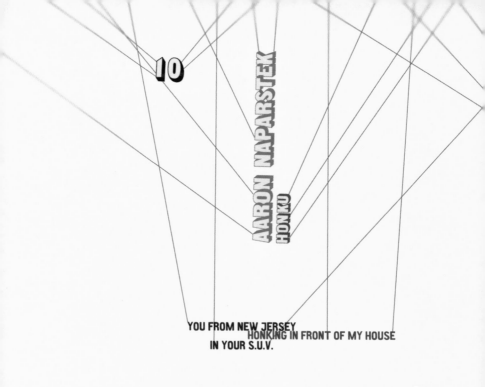

10

AARON NAPARSTEK
HONKU

YOU FROM NEW JERSEY
HONKING IN FRONT OF MY HOUSE
IN YOUR S.U.V.

Examples of this kind are sundry and often embarrassing—consider The Police's "He starts to shake and cough just like the old man in that book by Nabokov," and likely to make most authors feel stupid. On the other hand, writing your own lyrics is fun. And for this CD, absolutely the point since getting writers to moonlight as lyricists is a conflation that keeps with ORZ's aesthetic. Hell, Aaron Naparstek has a whole book of "honkus" that could work as songs, especially since this one is in 5/8, 7/8, 5/8, just like a haiku. Music nerds.

DENIS JOHNSON
BLESSING

CHRIST BY THE DUMPSTER PEELING AND TOSSING
YOUR LOTTERY TICKETS - OH NAZARENE DRINKING DUST, OH
CHRIST RISING AND FALLING, OH JESUS
CHRIST GIVING US THE FINGER IN "CHRIST AU TAMBEAU,"

BLESS PLEASE THE PEOPLE IN ART GALLERIES
LONELY AS A DISTANT TRAIN.
BLESS NOW
THE CANCER OF THE BONE, THE LAST LIGHT MAKING
BEAUTIFUL THE POISONS IN THE SKY-

AND THE CONDEMNED MAN IN HIS TUXEDO DREAM,
HIS DREAM OF LIMOUSINES AND INNOCENCE,
TAKE OFF YOUR CLOTHES AND COME TO HIM IN DREAMS.
STAND ON THE FIRE ESCAPE NAKED AND BLESS
WITH JAZZ LIKE A RIVULET OF CODEINE
THE LAUGHTER SPILLING FROM OUR BROKEN NECKLACES.

Thing is, **nerd** usually describes someone whose obsession–stamps, math, lepidoptery–crowds out the guy's ability to do much else, like dress well. Or switch hats. But ORZ, whose music often sticks to the creepy baseline, is considerably more versatile. At first, Denis Johnson said his lyrics were too country for the group. No problem. Herewith: a country song.

NEIL GAIMAN
ON THE WALL

SHE TOLD ME THAT
SHE DID NOT TRUST
AT ALL

THE ONES WHO DID NOT AGE
AND ADDED THAT
SHE KNEW SHE MUST
NOT FALL
UNTIL THE FINAL PAGE

I ONLY DREAMED
OF FALLING DOWN
THE NIGHT,
TILL I ENCOUNTERED YOU
AND ALL MY DREAMS
ARE UPSIDE DOWN

WE FIGHT

AND AFTER FIGHTING SCREW

-I TRUST THE ONES WHO DO NOT AGE
I DO NOT TRUST THE ONES WHO WAIT
AND UNDERSTAND THE ONES WHO DO
BUT DO NOT DO,
UNTIL TOO LATE.

-I THINK (I THINK I THINK I THINK)
THAT I WOULD RATHER RECOLLECT
A LIFE MISSPENT ON FRAGILE THINGS
THAN SPENT AVOIDING MORAL DEBT.
SHE WISHED ME WELL
AND WALKED AWAY
SHE SAW
THE WRITING ON THE WALL
THEN NOBODY WAS THERE AT ALL.

Followed by Neil Gaiman's torch ballad that appears to smile at one of those seventeenth-century seduction poems, a John Donne perhaps, while still invoking doom as its premise, the writing on the wall: **mene mene tekel parsin**. God has numbered the days of your kingdom and brought it to an end; you have been weighed on the scales and found wanting; your kingdom is divided and given. Well, shit. Then again, doesn't **mene mene tekel parsin** have precisely the aural and childlike qualities that make it work in a song, even as loose allusion? It's eenie meenie miney moe all over again.

13

AMY FUSSELMAN
ALL ABOUT HOUSE PLANTS

ALL THE PLANTS ARE ON FIRE
THEY HAVE A SECRET LIFE
ALL THE PLANTS ARE ON FIRE
THEY'RE LOOKING FOR A WIFE

ALL THEIR POTS HAVE TURNED TO GOLD
ALL THEIR LEAVES ARE ALMOST OLD

ALL THE PLANTS ARE ON FIRE
IN MY HOUSE IN THE RAIN

Likewise the talking plants. Wifeless, immolated, wizened, soused. People who talk to their plants are arguably more monstrous than people who sing alone in the shower because they don't really consider things from the plant's vantage. You might *think* you're keeping them company, but what you're **really** trying to do is mitigate the sort of loneliness that lands most people in the oven. Good thing this song is secretly about pogo sticks. Kids on pogo sticks. In the backyard, on a breezy afternoon as the sun casts halos on its loved ones.

MYLA GOLDBERG
GOLEM

SHOVEL ME SOME RED DIRT FULL OF KAOLINITE.
MOLD MYSELF A LOVER WHO'LL LAST MORE THAN ONE NIGHT.
IMPERTURBABILITY WILL BE YOUR BIRTHRIGHT;

SCRAWL MY NAME ACROSS YOUR HEAD.
I'LL TAKE UP WITH YOU INSTEAD.
PRETTIER THAN POETRY,
STRONGER THAN FIDELITY;
NO NEED FOR APOLOGY
WHEN YOU'RE MADE OF CLAY;
JUST AVOID THE RAINY DAYS.

DENSITY AND GRAVITY WILL KEEP YOU IN LINE.
MY DIRTY MAN, MY SEDIMENTAL VALENTINE.
KISSES PURE AS PORCELAIN AND CONDENSED SUNSHINE;
SETTLE DOWN BENEATH SOME TREES,
SQUEEZE US OUT A COUPLE TAR BABIES.

AGELESS AS ONTOLOGY,
HONEST AS GEOLOGY;
YOU'LL NEVER GROW TIRED OF ME
IF YOU'RE MADE OF CLAY;
JUST WATCH OUT FOR RAINY DAYS.

Not so the day ORZ recorded this song. Apparently, it was freezing. Which is nice to think about, given how sultry Syd Straw's voice can be. During the session, Michael and Joshua wrote Goldberg's flute line as they went along; it's true, she plays the flute. The extemporaneous gist of the process was something like: Is this too pretty? Let's mess it up. Which says a lot about what's going on here. Everything is too pretty until it's undead and reconfigured. Like Frankenstein's monster. Hermes and his woman. Even, well, a rock band.

15

A. M. HOMES

SNOW

FLAKES I CAUGHT IN THE PALM OF MY HAND
AND CARRIED IN TO MY MOTHER

TO REPLACE THE FADED DOILIES
UNDER THE LAMPS IN OUR LIVING ROOM

AT MY TEA PARTY
THE WHITE LACE TABLECLOTH MELTS
UNDER A CUP OF HOT CHOCOLATE

ORZ's studio is crammed with junk. Equipment and amps, sure, but also a bunch of junk. It's a mess down there. So it's particularly funny to think of them recording "Snow." Faded doilies would have made a nice addition to the place. That and a severed putty arm. I imagine the session might have had a little *Alice in Wonderland* in it. Like: Here we are in this dump at A. M. Homes's tea party. Eat some cake, outgrow your clothes. Nothing fits, and yet it's this not fitting, in its ugliness, that makes the music go.

THERE'S A FISH ON THE HOOK AND A LINE IN THE POND
BUT NOTHING ELSE IS HAPPENING HERE
WELL THAT OLD MOON IN THE SKY CASTS LIGHT ON THE GROUND
AND NOTHING ELSE IS HAPPENING HERE

WELL I CAN'T TAKE ANOTHER DAY
MY TONGUE IN MY MOUTH TASTES LIKE IT'S MADE OF CLAY
AND I CAN'T TAKE AN ANOTHER NIGHT
THE LION'S GOT HIS TEETH OUT BUT HE WON'T TAKE A BITE

WELL THE NIGHT AIR IS COLD AND HER HAIR'S A BRIGHT GOLD
IN MY DREAM YOU SEE I'M SOMETHING OF A KING
WELL WE'RE WALKING ON THE SAND HER HAND INSIDE MY HAND
AND ON THAT HAND SHE WEARS MY WEDDING RING

THERE'S A FISH ON THE HOOK AND A LINE IN THE POND
BUT NOTHING ELSE IS HAPPENING HERE
WELL THAT OLD MOON IN THE SKY CASTS LIGHT ON THE GROUND
BUT NOTHING ELSE IS HAPPENING HERE
NOTHING ELSE IS HAPPENING HERE.

For instance, who wants to be a writer sitting in some cottage in the woods? It's **too pretty**. The photographer Jill Krementz has a photo of E. B. White in a shack, sitting at a wooden desk in front of an old typewriter, silhouetted against a giant window that overlooks a lake. And, as Greenman tells us, nothing else is happening. So placid, that fish on the line. So placid, so dull.

JONATHAN AMES
THE STORY OF THE HAIRY CALL

WHEN I WAS A LITTLE BOY, I WAS VERY TROUBLED.

I HAD A BAD BACK AND AN ELEVATED TESTICLE.

I WAS EIGHT YEARS OLD.
I WASN'T EXACTLY OFF TO A GREAT START IN LIFE.
FOR MY BACK I HAD TO WEAR A CORSET.
FOR MY TESTICLE THERE WAS NOTHING TO DO BUT WAIT.

I'M A TRUMPET AND A WALL.
THIS IS THE STORY OF THE HAIRY CALL.

ONE DAY IN THE FOURTH GRADE JONATHAN "FAT" EDER MADE A SOUND.
A LITTLE PRAYER SOUND FROM THE BOTTOM OF HIS FAT BELLY.
HE WAS A NUTTY KID.

THE SON OF A CHIROPRACTOR.
SO HE MADE THIS SOUND AND IT WOKE ME UP.
AND IT WOKE UP ANOTHER BOY, FRANCIS "MANZI" MANZIANO.
THAT LITTLE SOUND.
KIND OF LIKE A SIGH, KIND OF LIKE A PURR, GREW INTO A LANGUAGE.

I'M A TRUMPET AND A WALL.
THIS IS THE STORY OF THE HAIRY CALL.

THE THREE OF US BECAME FRIENDS.
CALLED OURSELVES "THE HAIRIATORS."
SO THAT LITTLE SOUND GREW VERY LOUD.
WE LET IT LOOSE WHEN WE NEEDED EACH OTHER.
I'VE BEEN MAKING THAT SOUND EVER SINCE.

I'M A TRUMPET AND A WALL.
THIS IS THE STORY OF THE HAIRY CALL.

Course, E. B. White was the opposite of dull. He might have even had a little
Jonathan Ames in him, just waiting to get out. And wouldn't it be great if, in that
cottage of his, he too was writing about **nuts**? Nuts and the hairy call, which is what
I've been talking about all along. Everyone's got one. How you get from a mewl to the
thing Ames does at the end of this track might just be a matter of genetics. Or context.

18 JONATHAN LETHEM
WATER

AS SMART AS WE ARE
WE USE WATER AS A CLUE FOR FOOD
AS SMART AS WE ARE
WE GO MARCHING THROUGH THE DESERT

AS SMART AS WE ARE
WE USE WATER AS A CLUE FOR FOOD
WE GO MARCHING THROUGH THE DESERT

YOU FIND US IN THE BATHROOM
YOU FIND US IN THE SINK

YOU FIND US IN THE TOILET
HAVING OURSELVES A DRINK

WE USE WATER
AS A WAY OF SAYING THINGS WE DO NOT MEAN
WE USE WATER
AS A WAY OF LIVING FREE AND CLEAN
WE USE WATER
WE USE WATER AS OUR MIDDLE NAME
WE USE WATER
AS A WAY OF KEEPING EVERYTHING THE SAME

And context is everything. Apparently, Joshua and Michael accidentally wrote separate melodies for these lyrics. So they decided to alternate sections and mesh, which seems appropriately chaotic since no one had any idea what the song was about. As smart as we are, we have no idea what this song is about. We had to be told. It's about cockroaches. They will outlive us all. The dumbest of the plumb dumb, they will see the messiah.

CONTRIBUTING AUTHORS

JONATHAN AMES

IS THE AUTHOR OF *I PASS LIKE NIGHT; THE EXTRA MAN; WHAT'S NOT TO LOVE?; MY LESS THAN SECRET LIFE;* AND *WAKE UP, SIR!.* HE IS THE WINNER OF A GUGGENHEIM FELLOWSHIP AND HIS ONE-MAN SHOW OF STORYTELLING, "OEDIPUSSY," APPEARED OFF-OFF-BROADWAY. MR. AMES ALSO HAD A BRIEF FORAY AS BOXER, FIGHTING UNDER THE SOBRIQUET "THE HERRING WONDER," WHILE AMASSING A RECORD OF 0-1.

MARGARET ATWOOD

WAS BORN IN OTTAWA, ONTARIO ON NOVEMBER 18, 1939. SHE IS THE AUTHOR OF MORE THAN THIRTY-FIVE BOOKS, INCLUDING FICTION, POETRY, AND ESSAYS. AMONG HER MOST RECENT WORKS ARE THE BESTSELLING NOVELS *ORYX AND CRAKE; THE BLIND ASSASSIN; ALIAS GRACE; CAT'S EYE; THE HANDMAID'S TALE; THE ROBBER BRIDE,* AND THE COLLECTIONS *WILDERNESS TIPS* AND *BLUEBEARD'S EGG.*

AMONG THE MANY HONORS SHE HAS RECEIVED ARE THE BOOKER PRIZE, THE CANADIAN GOVERNOR GENERAL'S AWARD, THE SUNDAY TIMES AWARD FOR LITERARY EXCELLENCE IN THE UK, AND LE CHEVALIER DANS L'ORDRE DE ARTS ET LES LETTRES IN FRANCE. SHE LIVES IN TORONTO WITH THE NOVELIST GRAEME GIBSON.

PAUL AUSTER

IS THE AUTHOR OF ELEVEN NOVELS, INCLUDING *THE NEW YORK TRILOGY; LEVIATHAN; MR. VERTIGO; THE MUSIC OF CHANCE; TIMBUKTU; THE BOOK OF ILLUSIONS;* AND *ORACLE NIGHT.* HE LIVES IN BROOKLYN, NEW YORK.

CLAY MCLEOD CHAPMAN

FIRST BEGAN WRITING PLAYS AT THE AGE OF TWELVE. HE HAS DEVELOPED A STYLE OF CHARACTER MONOLOGUE THAT HE PERFORMS ONSTAGE AND TRANSFORMS TO THE PAGE.

HE HAS PERFORMED HIS "PUMPKIN PIE SHOW," A RIGOROUS STORYTELLING SESSION BACKED WITH ITS OWN LIVE SOUNDTRACK, THROUGHOUT THE UNITED STATES, AT THE ROMANIA INTERNATIONAL THEATER FESTIVAL, AND THE EDINBURGH FRINGE FESTIVAL. HE IS THE AUTHOR OF THE BOOKS *REST AREA* AND *MISS CORPUS*. HE LIVES IN BROOKLYN, NEW YORK.

DAVE EGGERS

IS THE EDITOR OF *McSWEENEY'S*, A QUARTERLY JOURNAL, AND HAS WRITTEN THREE BOOKS. *A HEARTBREAKING WORK OF STAGGERING GENIUS* WAS A FINALIST FOR THE PULITZER PRIZE AND HAS BEEN TRANSLATED INTO 17 LANGUAGES. *YOU SHALL KNOW OUR VELOCITY* WAS PUBLISHED LAST YEAR BY McSWEENEY'S BOOKS, AND WAS RELEASED IN PAPERBACK IN THE SUMMER OF 2003. EGGERS IS THE EDITOR OF *THE BEST AMERICAN NONREQUIRED READING*, WHICH HE CO-EDITS WITH STUDENTS FROM 826 VALENCIA, THE SAN FRANCISCO-BASED EDUCATIONAL NON-PROFIT HE CO-FOUNDED IN 2002.

DIMITRI EHRLICH

IS THE AUTHOR OF SEVERAL BOOKS, INCLUDING *INSIDE THE MUSIC: CONVERSATIONS WITH MUSICIANS ABOUT CREATIVITY, SPIRITUALITY AND CONSCIOUSNESS*. HIS WRITING HAS APPEARED IN PUBLICATIONS SUCH AS THE *NEW YORK TIMES*; *ROLLING STONE*; *SPIN*; *DETAILS*; *LONDON OBSERVER*; AND *INTERVIEW MAGAZINE*, WHERE HE SERVED AS MUSIC EDITOR FOR MANY YEARS AND IS NOW AN EDITOR AT LARGE. HE WROTE AND, ALONG WITH JANEANE GAROFALO, CO-HOSTED MTV'S *INDIE OUTING*. HE IS ALSO A SONGWRITER AND HAS RELEASED TWO CRITICALLY ACCLAIMED ALBUMS.

AMY FUSSELMAN

IS THE AUTHOR OF *THE PHARMACIST'S MATE*. SHE EDITS A WEB SITE CALLED "SURGERY OF MODERN WARFARE" AND IS THE MOTHER OF KING. SHE HAS BEEN IN SEVERAL ROCK BANDS, BUT NONE WITH A THEREMIN IN THEM.

NEIL GAIMAN

WRITES BESTSELLING BOOKS, IS ENGLISH, HAS WON MANY AWARDS, LIVES IN AMERICA, STILL WRITES COMICS FROM TIME TO TIME, AND FEEDS MANY CATS. NOT ALWAYS IN THAT ORDER.

NOT ONLY IS ## MYLA GOLDBERG THE AUTHOR OF *BEE SEASON*, BUT SHE ALSO PLAYS ACCORDION, BANJO, AND FLUTE. SHE LIVES IN BROOKLYN, NEW YORK, WITH HER HUSBAND, JASON LITTLE.

BEN GREENMAN

IS THE AUTHOR OF SEVERAL THINGS, SOME AS LONG AS BOOKS, SOME AS SHORT AS STORIES, SOME HILARIOUS AND OTHERS QUITE SAD, SOME PUBLISHED AROUND THE WORLD AND SOME STILL SITTING IN HIS DESK. AMONG THEM: A BOOK CALLED *SUPERBAD*, A BOOK CALLED *SUPERWORSE*, AND A STORY CALLED "IF I PUT MY FINGER AND MY THUMB TOGETHER I CAN FEEL THE WAY THE WORLD MUST FEEL SOME DAYS."

DANIEL HANDLER

IS THE AUTHOR OF THREE NOVELS: *THE BASIC EIGHT; WATCH YOUR MOUTH;* AND *ADVERBS,* AND IS MISTAKEN ON AN ALARMINGLY CONSISTENT BASIS FOR LEMONY SNICKET, THE AUTHOR OF NOVELS FOR CHILDREN KNOWN COLLECTIVELY AS *A SERIES OF UNFORTUNATE EVENTS.* THE SEMI-REGULAR ADJUNCT ACCORDIONIST FOR THE MAGNETIC FIELDS. MR. HANDLER LIVES IN SAN FRANCISCO WITH HIS CHARMING WIFE, LISA BROWN.

DENIS JOHNSON

IS THE AUTHOR OF *THE NAME OF THE WORLD; ALREADY DEAD; JESUS' SON; RESUSCITATION OF A HANGED MAN; FISKADORO; THE STARS AT NOON;* AND *ANGELS.* HIS POETRY HAS BEEN COLLECTED IN THE VOLUME *THE THRONE OF THE THIRD HEAVEN OF THE NATIONS MILLENNIUM GENERAL ASSEMBLY.* HE IS THE PLAYWRIGHT-IN-RESIDENCE FOR THE CAMPO SANTO THEATER GROUP IN SAN FRANCISCO AND THE COMPANY PLAYWRIGHT OF CHICAGO'S VIADUCT THEATER COMPANY.

INTERNATIONALLY ACCLAIMED – AND ALMOST ARRESTED –

A. M. HOMES

IS KNOWN FOR HER DARKLY COMIC NOVELS AND STORIES, AMONG THEM: *JACK; IN A COUNTRY OF MOTHERS; THE END OF ALICE;* AND *MUSIC FOR TORCHING,* THE ARTISTS' BOOK, *APPENDIX A:;* AND THE SHORT STORY COLLECTIONS, *THE SAFETY OF OBJECTS* AND *THINGS YOU SHOULD KNOW.* HER FICTION AND NONFICTION APPEAR FREQUENTLY IN MAGAZINES SUCH AS: *ART FORUM, HARPER'S, MCSWEENEY'S, THE NEW YORKER, THE NEW YORK TIMES MAGAZINE* AND *VANITY FAIR.* SHE IS THE RECIPIENT OF NUMEROUS AWARDS INCLUDING GUGGENHEIM AND NATIONAL ENDOWMENT FOR THE ARTS FELLOWSHIPS. SHE LIVES IN NEW YORK CITY, WHERE SHE SOMETIMES PERFORMS STANDUP COMEDY FOR HER FRIENDS AND NEIGHBORS.

"LAWRENCE KRAUSER"

IS THE PEN NAME OF DR. SALLY THIMBLETON, A NEW YORK-BASED PSYCHOANALYST WHOSE FIRST BOOK. *LEMON,* IS A COMPOSITE CASE STUDY DISTILLED FROM TWENTY-FIVE YEARS OF PROFESSIONAL PRACTICE. A FREQUENT GUEST COMMENTATOR ON DREAMS AND DYSPHORIA FOR FOX *MORNING NEWS,* SHE IS CURRENTLY ON SABBATICAL AT THE TWINE CENTER FOR THEOSOPHICAL REMEDY ON AVON MOUNTAIN, CONNECTICUT, COMPLETING A STUDY OF 20TH-CENTURY INDIGENOUS RELIGIONS OF MANHATTAN'S UPPER WEST SIDE.

JONATHAN LETHEM
IS THE AUTHOR OF *FORTRESS OF SOLITUDE*; *MOTHERLESS BROOKLYN*; *THIS SHAPE WE'RE IN*; *GUN, WITH OCCASIONAL MUSIC*; *GIRL IN LANDSCAPE*; *AS SHE CLIMBED ACROSS THE TABLE*; AND *AMNESIA MOON*. HE LIVES IN BROOKLYN.

FIONA MAAZEL
IS A SENIOR EDITOR AT *THE PARIS REVIEW*.

RICK MOODY
IS THE AUTHOR MOST RECENTLY OF *THE BLACK VEIL* AND *DEMONOLOGY*.

AARON NAPARSTEK
KNOWN BY SOME AS "THE BASHO OF HONK," IS A WRITER, WEB SITE PRODUCER AND TRANSPORTATION ACTIVIST IN BROOKLYN, NEW YORK. AFTER A NEAR-DEATH EGG-THROWING INCIDENT WITH AN INSANE MOTORIST, HE INVENTED HONKU, A NEW FORM OF POETRY, ANGER MANAGEMENT, AND COMMUNITY ACTIVISM. HE IS THE AUTHOR OF *HONKU: THE ZEN ANTIDOTE TO ROAD RAGE*.

DARIN STRAUSS
IS THE AWARD-WINNING AUTHOR OF THE BESTSELLING NOVELS *CHANG AND ENG* AND *THE REAL MCCOY*. HE TEACHES AT NYU AND LIVES IN BROOKLYN.

ONE RING ZERO *is:*

Joshua Camp: Vocals, accordion, claviola, Thomas organ, piano, keyboard, guitar, toy piano, banjo, and other noises.
Michael Hearst: Vocals, claviola, theremin, guitar, drums, bass, glockenspiel, slide whistle, and additional sounds.

PLUS:

Jonathan Ames: Hairy calls on 17
F.A. Blasco: Vocals on 16
Hanna Cheek: Vocals and banter on 7
Olivier Conan: Vocals on 9
Vincent Douglas: Lead guitar on 11
Brian Drye: Trombone on 14
Myla Goldberg: Flute on 14
Matt Grason: Bass on 5, 9
Allyssa Lamb: Vocals on 5
Anthony Mascorro: Trumpet on 2, 5, 8, 13, 18
Mike McGinnis: Clarinet on 14
Sean Moran: Slide guitar on 9
Sarah Noble: Cello on 12
Mark Snyder: Drum loop on 8
Darin Strauss: Guitar and backing vocals on 4
Syd Straw: Vocals on 14

All songs published by One Ring Zero Publishing, BMI.

© & ℗ 2004 One Ring Zero

Manager: Claudia Gonson
Music business consultant: Peter Wright
Packager: Sarah Sockit / Sockit Projects

Visit www.oneringzero.com.

One Ring Zero would like to thank the people who helped make this project possible. Unfortunately, we don't have room to print everyone's name here. Instead, please go to http://www.oneringzero.com/thankyou.htm.

This recording was engineered and produced by Michael Hearst and Joshua Camp on a 7 track reel-to-reel at Urban Geek Studios, Brooklyn, New York.

Introduction ©2004 ORZ
Natty Man Blues Lyrics ©2004 Paul Auster. Music ©2004 Michael Hearst and Joshua Camp.
Radio Lyrics ©2004 Daniel Handler. Music ©2004 Michael Hearst and Joshua Camp.
We Both Have A Feeling That You Still Want Me Lyrics ©2004 Darin Strauss. Music ©2004 Michael Hearst and Joshua Camp.
Kiss Me, You Brat Lyrics ©2004 Rick Moody. Music ©2004 Michael Hearst and Joshua Camp.
Deposition Disposition Lyrics ©2004 Lawrence Krauser. Music ©2004 Michael Hearst and Joshua Camp.
Half And Half Lyrics ©2004 Clay McLeod Chapman. Music ©2004 Michael Hearst and Joshua Camp.
The Ghost Of Rita Gonzalo Lyrics ©2004 Dave Eggers. Music ©2004 Michael Hearst and Joshua Camp.
Frankenstein Monster Song Lyrics ©2004 Margaret Atwood. Music ©2004 Michael Hearst and Joshua Camp.
Honku Lyrics ©2004 Aaron Naparstek. Music ©2004 Michael Hearst and Joshua Camp.
Blessing Lyrics ©2004 Denis Johnson. Music ©2004 Michael Hearst and Joshua Camp.
On The Wall Lyrics ©2004 Neil Gaiman. Music ©2004 Michael Hearst and Joshua Camp.
All About House Plants Lyrics ©2004 Amy Fusselman. Music ©2004 Michael Hearst and Joshua Camp.
Golem Lyrics ©2004 by Myla Goldberg. Music ©2004 Michael Hearst and Joshua Camp.
Snow Lyrics ©2004 by A.M. Homes. Music ©2004 Michael Hearst and Joshua Camp.
Nothing Else Is Happening Lyrics ©2004 Ben Greenman. Music ©2004 Michael Hearst and Joshua Camp.
The Story Of The Hairy Call Lyrics ©2004 Jonathan Ames. Music ©2004 Michael Hearst and Joshua Camp.
Water Lyrics ©2004 Jonathan Lethem. Music ©2004 Michael Hearst and Joshua Camp.